GETTING
GOSPEL RIGHT

GETTING THE GOSPEL RIGHT

Assessing the Reformation and New Perspectives on Paul

CORNELIS P. VENEMA

THE BANNER OF TRUTH TRUST

THE BANNER OF TRUTH TRUST
3 Murrayfield Road, Edinburgh EH12 6EL, UK
P.O. Box 621, Carlisle, PA 17013, USA

© Cornelis P. Venema 2006

ISBN-10: 0 85151 927 X
ISBN-13: 978 0 85151 927 2

Typeset in 11/15 pt Sabon at
the Banner of Truth Trust
Printed in the U.S.A. by
Versa Press, Inc.,
East Peoria, IL

CONTENTS

PREFACE

Every generation of Christian believers faces the challenge of proclaiming the gospel of Jesus Christ with integrity and in conformity with the teaching of the Scriptures.

At the time of the great Reformation of the church of Jesus Christ in the sixteenth century, this challenge was faced in an especially pressing way. When confronted with the teaching of the medieval Roman Catholic Church, the Reformers were compelled to protest against what they viewed as a profound misunderstanding of the gospel of God's grace in Christ.

Luther and Calvin, arguably the two greatest teachers of the Protestant Reformation, insisted that at the heart of the gospel lies the good news of God's gracious and free acceptance of guilty sinners on the basis of the obedience and atoning sacrifice of Christ.

The Roman Catholic teaching of justification by grace as well as meritorious good works had, in

their view, undermined this good news of free justification. And so they endeavoured to restore the
gospel of grace to its rightful place in the church's
understanding of the Scriptures. In doing so, they
found Paul's epistles, especially Galatians and
Romans, to be a primary source for the church's
proclamation of the good news of salvation through
Jesus Christ.

In recent decades, especially in the English-
speaking world, 'new perspectives' on the gospel
and the teaching of the apostle Paul have emerged
that challenge some of the basic tenets of the
Reformation's perspective. According to the authors
of the new perspectives, the Reformers' opposition
to the teaching of the medieval Roman Catholic
Church distorted their interpretation of Paul.

In their desire to proclaim the gospel of free
justification against their Catholic opponents, the
Reformers misread the apostle Paul's opposition to
the Judaizers of his day. The Reformers mistakenly
believed that Paul was opposing a Judaistic teaching
of salvation by works. Based upon their fresh study
of the historical sources, the authors of the newer
perspectives insist that Paul's doctrine of justification was aimed at a very different problem,
namely, the unwillingness of many Jewish believers

to admit Gentiles into the community of God's covenant people without obedience to certain 'boundary-marker' requirements of the law.

The purpose of this book is to offer a short summary of the important debate regarding the gospel that the newer perspectives on Paul have provoked. Since the new perspectives challenge some of the basic features of the traditional Protestant understanding of justification, they require careful study and thoughtful evaluation. Nothing less than the shape of the evangelical church's proclamation of the gospel today is at stake. The aim of this book is to offer a relatively brief introduction to the kind of study and evaluation of the new perspectives on Paul that is needed.

It should be noted that this book represents a condensed version of a much longer book on the subject that the Banner of Truth Trust has graciously consented to publish. Because it is a condensed version of this fuller treatment of the Reformation and new perspectives on the apostle Paul, many of the scriptural and theological arguments of the larger work have been either eliminated or greatly abbreviated. In a sense, this book offers only a skeleton of the larger work, and cannot stand alone. It is my hope, and I believe the hope of the Trust as well, that the reader will be encouraged to turn to the forthcoming larger book, in relation to which the present work is only a kind of outline of the subject.

Some of the material in this book was originally written as part of a lengthy series of articles in *The Outlook,* a Reformed periodical in North America that is written for a general audience. Though the book refers the reader to some of the academic literature on the newer perspectives, it is aimed at a general readership.

Since the newer perspectives on Paul have profound implications for the evangelical church's proclamation of the gospel in our time, it is only proper that evangelical believers and churches should be introduced to a discussion that is often intimidating because of its highly academic character.

Unless otherwise indicated, the Scripture quotations throughout the book are taken from the English Standard Version.

I am grateful for the assistance of Jonathan Watson of the Banner of Truth in the preparation of this book. It is my hope that it will contribute in some small way to a renewed appreciation for the gospel of God's free acceptance of his people in

Christ, and an informed awareness of the challenges to the evangelical church posed by the new perspectives on Paul and his understanding of the gospel.

CORNELIS P. VENEMA
March 2006

I

INTRODUCTION

I believe it was C. S. Lewis who, commenting on the modern temptation to innovate in matters of worship and theology, wryly observed, 'Fashions come and go, but mostly they go.' Lewis's point was clear enough: the Christian church, whose worship and theology represent the fruit of centuries of reflection upon Scripture, needs to beware of the contemporary fascination with the new and trendy.

If the catholicity of the church means anything, it means that the church should cultivate a profound respect for its inheritances in the faith, and look with suspicion upon present-day theological fads.

Christian believers who stand in the tradition of the Protestant Reformation need to remember

Lewis's warning when it comes to the subject of this study, the 'new perspective(s) on the apostle Paul'.[1]

Though Protestant believers are committed to the principle of *sola Scriptura*, which requires a continual process of testing theological trends by the standard of Scripture, they must not confuse reformation according to the Word of God with fascination for new views simply because they are new.

One of the great challenges facing the contemporary church, then, is the emergence of a new perspective on Paul, which claims to offer a more satisfactory interpretation of Paul's understanding of the gospel of free justification than that of the sixteenth-century Reformers. By any measure this is

---

[1] The expression, 'new perspective on Paul', was coined by James D. G. Dunn in an early article on the subject. See Dunn, 'The New Perspective on Paul', in *Jesus, Paul and the Law: Studies in Mark and Galatians* (Louisville, KY: Westminster/John Knox Press, 1990), pp. 183–214. Proponents and opponents of a newer way of interpreting Paul have noted that we should more accurately speak of new 'perspectives' on Paul. See e.g. N. T. Wright, 'New Perspectives on Paul', http://home.hiwaay.net/~kbush/Wright_New_Perspectives.pdf; and Guy Prentiss Waters, *Justification and the New Perspectives on Paul: A Review and Response* (Phillipsburg, NJ: Presbyterian & Reformed, 2004).

a bold claim. And it unavoidably confronts believers with the question: Is this new view of Paul's teaching one that will prove lasting, or is it a view that will soon be seen only in the rear-view mirror of theology? Does it represent a substantial change in the way contemporary believers should understand Paul's teaching, or is it a passing fad?

I am convinced that the new perspective on Paul demands the attention of contemporary believers, especially Protestants whose understanding of the gospel has been shaped by the great Reformation of the church in the sixteenth century. Since the new perspective challenges some of the most basic features of the Protestant understanding of the gospel of free justification, it can scarcely be ignored. My primary purpose in this study, therefore, will be to introduce the new perspective on Paul.

This summary of the new perspective begins with a brief sketch of the main tenets of the historic Protestant perspective on Paul. This sketch will provide a context for our consideration of the new perspective.

The bulk of the study will summarize and evaluate the new perspective itself, considering three significant figures in its development.

Following the summary of the new perspective's main features, the remainder of the study will offer a critical assessment of its claims. While acknowledging helpful aspects of the new perspective, this assessment concludes that it does not finally offer a better reading of the writings of the apostle Paul than that of the sixteenth-century Reformers.

2

THE REFORMATION
PERSPECTIVE
ON PAUL

Before directly taking up the new perspective on Paul, we need to consider the historic Protestant understanding of justification.

In the literature on the new perspective, references are frequently made to the old perspective on Paul, which presumably means the predominant view of the Protestant Reformation of the sixteenth century. We seldom find, however, any sustained treatment of the doctrine of justification that was advocated by the Reformers. Assumptions are made regarding the shape of the traditional Protestant view, but these are frequently left unexamined or presented without citations from the principal authors and confessions of the period. Since the new perspective presents itself as an alternative to the older perspective, a critical assessment of the new perspective requires an accurate understanding of the Reformation perspective from which it is distinguished. Though this abbreviated study is not able to present a thorough account of the Reformation's doctrine of justification,[2] we need to note some of its important emphases.

When considering the older perspective on Paul's doctrine of justification, we must be careful to state

---

[2] For more complete summaries of the Reformation doctrine of justification, see John Calvin, *Institutes* III.xi; James Buchanan, *The Doctrine of Justification* (1867; repr. London: Banner of Truth, 1961); G. C. Berkouwer, *Faith and Justification* (Grand Rapids: Eerdmans, 1954); Robert Traill, *Justification Vindicated* (1692; rev. ed., Edinburgh: Banner of Truth, 2002; James R. White, *The God Who Justifies* (Minneapolis: Bethany House, 2001); Anthony N. S. Lane, *Justification by Faith in Catholic-Protestant Dialogue: An Evangelical Assessment* (London: T. & T. Clark, 2002) pp. 17–44; John Owen, *Works*, vol. 5: *The Doctrine of Justification by Faith* (1850–53; repr. London: Banner of Truth, 1965); Francis Turretin, *Institutes of Elenctic Theology* (Phillipsburg, NJ: Presbyterian & Reformed, 1994), 2:633–88; and Alister E. McGrath, *Iustitia Dei: A History of the Christian Doctrine of Justification* (2nd ed., New York: Cambridge University Press, 1986, 1998), pp. 188–240.

its understanding as clearly as possible. Saying merely that believers are 'justified by grace through faith' does not adequately state the Protestant view.[3] In the classic Protestant view, believers are said to be justified before God *by grace alone* (*sola gratia*) on account of the work of *Christ alone* (*solo Christo*), and this free justification becomes theirs *by faith alone* (*sola fide*).

Each of these expressions is an essential part of the Reformation's understanding of justification. In our summary of the older Protestant understanding of justification, therefore, we will successively treat each of these phrases in the traditional formulation. The questions we need to answer are: (1) What did

[3] This formulation is used in a recent declaration, 'Evangelicals and Catholics Together', which was signed by North American evangelical and Roman Catholic representatives. For an evangelical critique of this declaration, see R. C. Sproul, *Faith Alone: The Evangelical Doctrine of Justification* (Grand Rapids: Baker, 1995). For an extended evaluation of recent ecumenical discussions on the doctrine of justification, see Anthony N. S. Lane, *Justification by Faith in Catholic-Protestant Dialogue: An Evangelical Assessment*. One frequently overlooked, feature of the new perspective is its claim that a fresh reading of the apostle Paul's doctrine of justification will show that it is an 'ecumenical' doctrine that should unite rather than divide the Christian churches.

the Reformers understand by the terminology of 'justification'? (2) Why did they insist that this justification is 'by grace alone' on account of the work of 'Christ alone'? And (3) why did they also insist that the gracious justification of believers becomes theirs 'by faith alone'?

1. 'JUSTIFICATION': A JUDICIAL DECLARATION OF ACCEPTANCE WITH GOD

One common way of expressing the nature of the Protestant understanding of justification is by noting that it views justification as a *forensic* or *judicial* declaration of God. Unlike the classic Roman Catholic doctrine, which regards justification as including a *moral process* or *transformation* of believers, the Protestant conception identifies justification with the pronouncement of the believer's innocence in God's court. According to the Reformation view, justification is a legal declaration by God, which pronounces the justified person righteous or acceptable to him.[4] The antonym of

---

[4] The definition of justification in the *Westminster Larger Catechism,* Q. & A. 70, is typical: 'Justification is an act of God's free grace unto sinners, in which he pardoneth all

justification, accordingly, is 'condemnation' or being declared guilty (*Rom.* 8:33–34). By contrast, the Roman Catholic view maintains that justification includes a process of moral transformation equivalent to what, in evangelical terms, is known as the work of sanctification.[5]

Though the language of justification is metaphorical, depicting sinners in legal terms as persons called to appear before God as their Judge, for the Reformers this language represented the real (or literal) situation of all persons in relation to God.

---

their sins, accepteth and accounteth their persons righteous in his sight; not for any thing wrought in them, or done by them, but only for the perfect obedience and full satisfaction of Christ, by God imputed to them, and received by faith alone' (quoted from *Ecumenical Creeds and Reformed Creeds and Confessions,* classroom edition; Orange City, IA: Mid-America Reformed Seminary, 1991).

[5] Cf. the definition of justification in the *Canons and Decrees of the Council of Trent*, Sixth Session, Chapter 7 (quoted from Philip Schaff, *The Creeds of Christendom* [1931; repr. Grand Rapids: Baker, 1985, 2:94): 'This disposition, or preparation, is followed by Justification itself, which is not remission of sins merely, but also the sanctification and renewal of the inward man, through the voluntary reception of the grace, and of the gifts, whereby man of unjust becomes just [*fit iustus*] . . .'

As creatures originally created in God's image, but now fallen into sin in Adam, all human beings are accountable before God (*Rom.* 2–3). So far as the Reformers were concerned, the problem that justification addresses can hardly be exaggerated. To be hailed before a human court and adjudged innocent or guilty is a matter of some importance. But to be hailed before God and to be subject to his judgment, is a matter of ultimate importance.

Consequently, the Reformers regarded the question of justification, not as one question among many, but as *the* religious question, the paramount question in life and in death.

The justification of believers is a definitive act, which declares them guiltless before God and forgives them their sins. In the Reformation understanding of the gospel, justification is the principal benefit of Christ's saving work, revealing God's grace toward undeserving sinners whom he saves from condemnation and death (*Rom.* 5:12–21).

In this perspective on the gospel, justification is a thoroughly theological and soteriological theme, which reveals God's righteousness and his deliverance of sinners from their sinful plight.

2. 'BY GRACE ALONE': THE BASIS FOR FREE JUSTIFICATION

Though the Reformers believed that the Roman Catholic view confused justification and sanctification by treating justification as though it involved a process of moral renewal, this was not their basic complaint against it. According to the Reformers, the basic error of Roman Catholicism resides in its wrong conception of *the foundation* of this verdict.

In Roman Catholic teaching, God justifies believers in part on the basis of their own righteousness. Because justification includes a process of moral renewal, the righteousness that justifies believers is said to be an inherent righteousness (*iustitia inhaerens*).[6] When God justifies believers, he does not do so solely upon the basis of the work and merits of Christ, which are granted and

---

[6] Cf. Schaff, *The Creeds of Christendom*, 2:95–6: 'For, although no one can be just, but he to whom the merits of the Passion of our Lord Jesus Christ are communicated, yet is this done in the said justification of the impious, when by the merit of that same most holy Passion, *the charity of God is poured forth*, by the Holy Spirit, *in the hearts* of those that are justified, and is inherent therein [*atque ipsis inhaeret*].'

imputed to believers by grace, but partly upon the basis of the work and merits of believers, which are the fruit of God's grace at work in them.[7]

In their protest against this Roman Catholic understanding of the basis for the justification of believers, the Reformers insisted that justification is wholly a free gift of God's grace. Grace alone – not grace plus the working of believers prompted by grace – is the exclusive basis for the justification and salvation of believers. So far as their acceptance with God is concerned, believers rest their confidence, not in anything they might do in obedience to God, but in God's gracious favour demonstrated in the free provision of redemption through Jesus Christ.

Consequently, the Reformers emphasized that the righteousness justifying believers is an 'alien' and 'imputed' righteousness (*iustitia aliena et imputata*),

---

[7] *The Canons and Decrees of the Council of Trent*, Sixth Session, Chapter 10 (Schaff, *The Creeds of Christendom*, 2:99). This has two serious and acknowledged consequences: first, Christ alone is no longer the believer's righteousness before God; and second, the believer cannot have any assurance of salvation (unless by special dispensation and revelation) since his own righteousness can scarcely provide any sure footing in the presence of God.

not a personal or inherent righteousness. Though this language is often criticized for suggesting that justification involves a kind of 'legal fiction', the Reformers used it in order to emphasize that the believer's justification rests upon the righteousness of another, namely, Jesus Christ.

By means of his suffering and death on the cross, Christ bore the penalty and suffered the curse of the law on behalf of his people. Christ satisfied God's justice by his endurance of the condemnation and death that properly are due to those who violate the law of God.

Furthermore, by means of his obedience and fulfilment of all the requirements of the law, Christ met all the demands of righteousness on their behalf. Christ alone, upon the basis of his obedience to and satisfaction of the law's demands, secures the justification of his people.[8]

[8] Cf. Louis Berkhof's definition of justification in his *Systematic Theology* (London: Banner of Truth, 1958), p. 513: 'Justification is a judicial act of God, in which He declares, on the basis of the righteousness of Jesus Christ, that all the claims of the law are satisfied with respect to the sinner.' Traditional Reformed theology distinguished in this connection between the 'active' and 'passive' obedience of Christ. The purpose of this distinction was not to divide Christ's obedience into two chronological stages (the first

Consistent with this understanding of the basis for the justification of believers, the Reformers sharply distinguished between the law and the gospel in relation to justification. When distinguished from the gospel, the law of God refers to the righteous requirements that God imposes upon human beings as his image-bearers.

Whether Jews, who received the law of God in written form through Moses, or Gentiles, who have the works of the law written upon their consciences, all human beings fail to live in perfect conformity to the law's demands (*Rom.* 2–3). By the standard of the perfect law of God, all human beings stand condemned and are worthy of death as the wages of sin (*Rom.* 6:23).

---

being his earthly ministry, the second being his sacrificial death upon the cross) or even into two parts, but to distinguish two facets of the one obedience of Christ. Christ's active obedience refers to his life of conformity to the precepts of the law; Christ's passive obedience refers to his life of suffering under the penalty of the law, especially in his crucifixion (*Rom.* 5:12–21; *Phil.* 2:5ff; *Gal.* 4:4). For traditional presentations of this distinction and its significance for justification, see Berkhof, *Systematic Theology*, pp. 379–82, 513ff.; Turretin, *Institutes of Elenctic Theology*, pp. 646–59; Buchanan, *The Doctrine of Justification*, pp. 314–38.

Though the law of God is good and holy, it can only demand from believers what they cannot do. No one can be justified by the works of the law because no one actually does perfectly what the whole law requires.

Contrary to the law's function of exposing human sin and guilt, the gospel proclaims the good news that God freely grants to believers in Christ what the law could never achieve: acceptance and favour with himself on account of the righteousness of Christ.

Since the righteousness that is imputed to believers is not their own righteousness, but the righteousness of Christ, the Reformers also spoke of the justified person as *simul iustus et peccator*, 'at once just and a sinner'. This expression was a deliberately provocative one, since it called attention to the sharp difference between the Roman Catholic view that sinners are *made* righteous and the Reformation view that sinners are *declared* righteous.

By using this language, the Reformers emphasized that the grace of free justification involves the justification of the *ungodly* (*iustificatio impii*, Rom. 4:5), and not the godly. Justification reveals the sheer grace of God who receives and welcomes sinners in spite of their utter unworthiness. Full acceptance with God does not wait for the full transformation of believers into righteous people.

Full acceptance with God is found in Christ whose righteousness is perfectly adequate to the need of believers. To say that a believer is 'at once just and a sinner', therefore, is to affirm that human sinfulness is not an insuperable obstacle to God's free grace. Grace triumphs in the gospel of free justification, even in the face of continued human sinfulness and unworthiness.

3. 'THROUGH FAITH ALONE': THE INSTRUMENT OF JUSTIFICATION

The Protestant insistence that believers are justified by faith alone was an obvious corollary of the Reformation's insistence that justification is a free gift of God's grace in Christ. If justification is a free gift, which is based upon a righteousness graciously granted and imputed to believers, it most emphatically is not by works. 'Grace alone', 'Christ alone', and 'faith alone', are corollary expressions. To say one is to say the others. If we are saved by grace alone, then works must be excluded as a necessary precondition for our being accepted into favour with God. If we are saved by the Person and work of Christ alone, then nothing believers do before God in obedience to the law could possibly complete or compensate for anything lacking in this salvation. According to the Reformers, this is precisely what the language of 'faith alone' asserts.

To express the unique suitability of faith to receive the gift of free justification, the Reformers used a variety of expressions. Calvin, for example, spoke of faith as an 'empty vessel' in order to stress its character as a receptacle that brings nothing to God but receives all things from him.[9] Luther used the striking analogy of a ring that clasps a jewel; faith has no value of itself, but clasps the jewel that is Christ and his righteousness.[10] Calvin also remarked that, in a manner of speaking, faith is a 'passive thing', because it is the cessation of all working and striving to obtain favour and acceptance with God in order to rest in a favour freely given in Christ.[11] What makes faith a suitable

[9] *Institutes of the Christian Religion* (ed. John T. McNeill), Philadelphia: Westminster Press, 1960), III.xi.7.

[10] *Luther's Works* (American Edition, ed. Jaroslav Pelikan and Helmut T. Lehmann), St. Louis: Concordia Publishing House, and Philadelphia: Fortress Press, 1955–86), vol. 26, p. 89, 134.

[11] *Institutes*, III.xiii.5.

instrument for the reception of free justification is that it is marked by a humble acknowledgement that all honour in salvation belongs to God in Christ. As a receptive and passive acknowledgement of the sheer graciousness of free justification, faith is an act of trustful acceptance of what God freely grants believers in Christ. When believers accept the free gift of justification by faith, they look away from themselves and focus their attention upon Christ who is their righteousness.

Faith is the antithesis of any boasting in human achievement before God. Because such faith finds its sufficiency in Christ's saving work, it also produces a confident assurance of his favour.[12]

---

[12] It should be noted that the 'faith-alone' formulation of the Reformers is not meant to imply that faith, which is the exclusive instrument of justification, is a lonely or work-less faith. According to the Reformers, true faith always produces fruits in good works. Cf. Calvin's well-known comment in his 'Canons and Decrees of the Council of Trent, with the Antidote', in *Selected Works of John Calvin: Tracts and Letters* (ed. Henry Beveridge, 1851; repr. Grand Rapids: Baker Book House, 1983), 3:152: 'It is therefore faith alone which justifies, and yet the faith which justifies is not alone; just as it is the heat alone of the sun which warms the earth, and yet in the sun it is not alone, because it is constantly conjoined with light.'

KEY FEATURES OF THE REFORMATION PERSPECTIVE

Now that we have briefly considered the Reformation perspective on justification, we are in a position to delineate several of its features that are of special importance to the new perspective on Paul.

When authors of the new perspective contrast their understanding of Paul with the older perspective, these distinctive features of the Reformation view are often singled out for criticism.

FIRST, *the Reformation perspective views justification as a principal theme of the gospel of Jesus Christ.*

Because justification answers the question of how guilty sinners can find acceptance with God, it belongs to the heart of the Christian gospel and is a central theme in the writings of the apostle Paul.

Though the gospel embraces more within its scope than the truth of free justification, this article is regarded as the article of 'the standing or the falling of the church', to use the language of Lutheranism, or the 'main hinge' of the Christian religion, to use the language of John Calvin.

SECOND, *the Reformation understanding of justification maintains that it is a primarily theological and soteriological theme.*

On the one hand, justification reveals the character of God as a God of righteousness and grace, who justifies ungodly sinners on the basis of the work of Christ. On the other hand, justification reveals the character of sinful humans who can only be received and accepted by God on the basis of the righteousness of Christ alone.

In this respect, justification is a thoroughly soteriological theme, which explains how otherwise guilty sinners can be received into God's favour.

THIRD, *the Reformation perspective on justification claims that the medieval Roman Catholic doctrine of justification compromised the gospel by emphasizing obedience to the law as a partial, meritorious basis for justification.*

According to the Reformers' reading of the apostle Paul, this error of Roman Catholic teaching was similar in form to the error of the Pharisees and Judaizers in Paul's day. Just as the apostle Paul opposed the erroneous view of those who claimed to find favour with God on the basis of their meritorious works, so the Reformers in their day claimed to be opposing a similar error in Catholicism. Luther especially emphasized the essential similarity between the Roman Catholic teaching of salvation by meritorious good works and the Pharisaical or Judaizing teaching of salvation by obedience to the law of God. But Calvin also charged the Roman Catholic Church with the same error that had earlier characterized the religion of the Pharisees and Judaism.[13]

FOURTH, *the Reformation perspective insists that, when Paul speaks of 'works' or 'works of the law', he refers to any acts of obedience to the law, which are regarded as the basis for acceptance with God.*

When Paul opposes those who boasted of their works, he opposes those who claimed to find favour with God on the basis of their own righteousness, which was exhibited in their obedience to the law. Part of Paul's argument is that no one is able to do

---

[13] Calvin, for example, in his commentary on Philippians 3:8, spoke of the Roman Catholics of his time as 'present-day Pharisees' who uphold 'their own merits against Christ'. See *Calvin's New Testament Commentaries: Galatians, Ephesians, Philippians and Colossians*, ed. David W. Torrance and Thomas F. Torrance (Grand Rapids: Eerdmans, 1965), 11:274.

what the law requires, and this inability illustrates the contrast between the law and the gospel.

And FIFTH, the Reformers viewed the righteousness of God, which is revealed in the gospel of Jesus Christ, as something that God freely grants and imputes to believers.

For Luther and Calvin, the righteousness of God was not identified with the severe demand of the law, but with the gracious act whereby God grants believers a share in the righteousness of Christ.

When God grants the righteousness of Jesus Christ to believers, they enjoy the grace of acceptance or a right standing with him.

3

A 'NEW PERSPECTIVE' ON PAUL

The Reformation perspective on Paul's doctrine of justification largely dominated Protestant biblical scholarship in the following centuries. However, the last two hundred years of critical biblical studies of the apostle Paul's writings have witnessed a number of attempts to revisit the Reformation consensus. Within the orbit of the academic study of Paul, two particular questions have frequently surfaced in evaluating the Reformation view.

FIRST, *is the doctrine of justification as central a theme in Paul's understanding of the gospel as the Reformation perspective suggests*, or should a different theme be identified as the dominant feature of Paul's preaching?

And SECOND, *was Paul's relationship with his ancestral religion, Judaism, as uniformly negative as traditional Protestant theology supposed?*

Each of these questions has profound implications for determining whether the Reformation perspective represents an accurate interpretation of Paul's understanding of the gospel.

If the 'centre' of Paul's theology is 'mystical union' with the crucified and risen Christ, rather than the gracious justification of sinners, the Reformation reading of the apostle may reflect an undue narrowing of the scope of Paul's teaching.[14]

Or, if the gospel Paul preached was a fulfilment rather than a repudiation of Judaism, the Reformation's emphasis upon Paul's dispute with 'Judaizers', who were teaching a form of salvation by the works of the law, may likewise be a misreading of Paul's teaching. The emergence of the new perspective can be viewed as the direct result of

---

[14] Albert Schweitzer, *The Mysticism of Paul the Apostle* (New York: Holt, 1931), p. 225, expressed this view when he concluded that Paul's forensic language is subordinate to his 'mystical doctrine of redemption through the being-in-Christ'.

the investigation of precisely these kinds of questions.[15]

The story of the emergence of the new perspective within modern scholarship lies outside of the scope of this study. Since my aim is to provide a simple sketch of the new perspective, I will restrict the discussion to a delineation of its most important emphases.

While the new perspective encompasses a wide variety of viewpoints, there are especially three claims that recur throughout a great deal of the literature on the subject.

The FIRST CLAIM is that *the Reformation view of justification was built upon the foundation of a false picture of Judaism at the time of the writing of Paul's epistles.*

The SECOND CLAIM is that *the Reformation view of justification improperly identified the problem to which Paul's doctrine of justification was addressed, when it took his language about the 'works of the law' to refer to a kind of legalistic righteousness.*

The THIRD CLAIM is that *the language of 'justification' in Paul's epistles does not primarily refer to*

[15] See Waters, *Justification and the New Perspectives on Paul*, pp. 1–33.

*the way guilty sinners find acceptance with God,
but to the identification of who belongs to the
covenant people of God.*

In our treatment of these claims, we will illustrate
how each of these themes has been advanced in the
writings of three important architects of the new
perspective on Paul.

A NEW VIEW OF
SECOND-TEMPLE JUDAISM:
E. P. SANDERS

Even though the new perspective has roots in Pauline
studies that go back at least two centuries, the more
immediate beginning of the story of this perspective
starts with the influential work of E. P. Sanders.[16]

In 1977, Sanders published a volume, *Paul and
Palestinian Judaism*. This is now generally regarded
as a classic presentation of the view of Second-
Temple Judaism which is basic to the new

---

[16] For helpful surveys of the background to the new
perspective in New Testament and Pauline studies, see
Stephen Westerholm, *Perspectives Old and New on Paul:
The 'Lutheran' Paul and His Critics* (Grand Rapids:
Eerdmans, 2004), pp. 101–49 and 178–200, and Waters,
Justification and the New Perspectives on Paul, pp. 1–33.

perspective.[17] Sanders' stated purpose in his classic study was to compare the pattern of religion evident in Paul's writings with the pattern of religion in Jewish literature during the period between 200 B.C. and A.D. 200.

By a 'pattern of religion', Sanders means the way a religion understands how a person 'gets in' and 'stays in' the community of God's people.[18] Traditional accounts of the differences between religions, particularly the differences between Judaism and Christianity, focused upon the distinctive essence or core beliefs of these religions. In doing so, Judaism was often simplistically described as a 'legalistic' religion, which emphasizes obedience to the law as the basis for inclusion among God's people, and Christianity was described as a 'gracious' religion, which emphasizes God's free initiative in calling his people into communion with himself.

In the first part of his study, Sanders provides a comprehensive survey of Jewish literature during the two centuries before and after the coming of Christ. On the basis of this survey, Sanders maintains that Second-Temple Judaism exhibits a

[17] Philadelphia: Fortress Press, 1977.
[18] *Paul and Palestinian Judaism*, p. 17.

pattern of religion best described as 'covenantal nomism'. Sanders defines covenantal nomism as follows:

> The 'pattern' or 'structure' of covenantal nomism is this: (1) God has chosen Israel and (2) given the law. The law implies both (3) God's promise to maintain the election and (4) the requirement to obey. (5) God rewards obedience and punishes transgression. (6) The law provides for means of atonement, and atonement results in (7) maintenance or re-establishment of the covenantal relationship. (8) All those who are maintained in the covenant by obedience, atonement and God's mercy belong to the group which will be saved. An important interpretation of the first and last points is that election and ultimately salvation are considered to be by God's mercy rather than human achievement.[19]

Whereas the traditional Protestant view claimed that Palestinian Judaism was legalistic, Sanders appeals to evidence in Jewish writings of the Second-Temple period to support the view that it was fundamentally a religion of grace. In the literature of Judaism, God is represented as graciously

[19] *Paul and Palestinian Judaism*, p. 422.

electing Israel to be his people, and mercifully providing a means of atonement and opportunity for repentance in order to deal with their sins. So far as Israel's 'getting in' the covenant is concerned, this was not by human achievement but by God's gracious initiative. Obedience to the law was only required as a means of maintaining or 'staying in' the covenant.

One of the immediate questions raised by Sanders' new view of Judaism is: What explains the apostle Paul's opposition to Judaism? If Judaism was not a legalistic religion, what are we to make of Paul's vigorous arguments against claims to find favour with God on the basis of works? Is Paul combatting a kind of 'straw man' in his letters (especially in Romans and Galatians), when he combats a righteousness that is by the 'works of the law'?

Sanders, both in his *Paul and Palestinian Judaism* and in a sequel, *Paul, the Law, and the Jewish People*,[20] answers this question by suggesting that Paul's view of the human plight was a by-product of his view of salvation. Paul started with Christ as the 'solution' to the human predicament, and then

[20] Minneapolis: Fortress Press, 1983.

worked backward to explain the 'plight' to which his saving work corresponds.

Though Paul has traditionally been interpreted as teaching that the problem of human sinfulness is made known through the law's demand for perfect obedience, we should recognize that his description of the problem of sin actually stems from his prior convictions about Christ.

Paul starts from the basic conviction that Christ is the only Saviour of Jews and Gentiles. Upon the basis of this prior conviction, he then develops a doctrine of the law and human sinfulness that corresponds to it. According to Sanders, the great problem with Judaism, so far as the apostle Paul was concerned, was not that it was legalistic. Paul's principal objection to Judaism was that it rejected the new reality of God's saving work through Christ.

In words that have often been quoted, Sanders concludes: 'In short, *this is what Paul finds wrong in Judaism: it is not Christianity.*'[21]

---

[21] *Paul and Palestinian Judaism*, p. 552. Cf. Sanders' comment on p. 497: 'It is the Gentile question and the exclusivism of Paul's soteriology which dethrone the law, not a misunderstanding of it or a view predetermined by his background.'

A NEW VIEW OF THE 'WORKS OF THE LAW': JAMES D. G. DUNN

In addition to the claim that the Reformation perspective on Paul was mistakenly built upon a wrong view of Judaism, the new perspective also claims that it was built upon a misunderstanding of Paul's view of the 'works of the law'.

Among authors who advocate a new perspective on Paul, James D. G. Dunn, who teaches New Testament at the University of Durham, England, has particularly argued for this aspect of the new approach.[22]

---

[22] Among the more important sources for an understanding of Dunn's view are his books and articles, as follows:

'The New Perspective on Paul', in *Jesus, Paul and the Law: Studies in Mark and Galatians* (Louisville: Westminster/John Knox Press, 1990), pp. 183–215;

'Paul and "covenantal nomism"', in *The Partings of the Ways between Christianity and Judaism and Their Significance for the Character of Christianity* (Philadelphia: Trinity Press International, 1991), pp. 117–139;

'Works of the Law and the Curse of the Law (Galatians 3.10–14)', *New Testament Studies*, 31 (1985): 523–42;

The Theology of Paul the Apostle (Grand Rapids: Eerdmans, 1998), pp. 334–89;

In a 1982 lecture, 'The New Perspective on Paul', Dunn acknowledged that Sanders' study, *Paul and Palestinian Judaism*, called for a 'new pattern' for understanding the apostle Paul. In this lecture, Dunn credited Sanders with breaking the stranglehold of the older Reformation view that had dominated Pauline studies for centuries.[23]

The idea that there is a basic antithesis between Judaism, which supposedly taught a doctrine of salvation by meritorious works, and Paul, who taught a doctrine of salvation by faith apart from the works of the law, needs, Dunn believes, to be set aside once and for all.

Judaism, as Sanders had convincingly demonstrated, was a religion of salvation that emphasized God's goodness and generosity toward his people, Israel. The law was given to Israel, not as a means of procuring favour with God, but as a means of confirming the covenant relationship previously established by grace.

Word Biblical Commentary, vol. 38a: *Romans 1–8*, and vol. 38b: *Romans 9–16* (Dallas: Word Books, 1988);

'Yet Once More — "The Works of the Law": A Response', *Journal for the Study of the New Testament*, 46 (1992): 99–117.

[23] 'The New Perspective on Paul', p. 184.

In spite of Sanders' ground-breaking insights, Dunn claims that he failed to provide a coherent explanation of Paul's relation to Judaism.

Though Sanders' new view of Judaism provided the occasion for a new perspective on Paul, the interpretation of Paul's gospel he adopted fails to show how Paul's view of the law arose within the Judaism of his day. If the problem with Judaism's understanding of the law was not legalism, which teaches that obedience to the law's requirements is the basis for inclusion among God's covenant people, we need to press the question: What was wrong with its teaching? To what error is the apostle Paul responding, when he speaks of a justification that is not according to 'works of the law' but according to faith?

If we approach the apostle Paul from the perspective of the new view of Judaism, we will discover, Dunn argues, that Paul was objecting to *Jewish exclusivism* and not legalism.

The problem with the use of the law among the Judaizers whom Paul opposed was not their attempt to find favour with God on the basis of their obedience to the law, but their use of the 'works of the law' to exclude Gentiles from membership in the covenant community.

The Judaizers were insisting upon certain 'works of the law' that served as 'boundary-markers' for inclusion or exclusion from the number of God's people. The law functioned in their practice as a means of identifying who properly belongs to the community of faith. It was this *social* use of the law as a means of excluding Gentiles that receives Paul's rebuke, not an alleged appeal to the law as a means of self-justification.

According to Dunn, Paul's real objection to the Judaizers' appeal to the 'works of the law' is clearly disclosed in passages like Galatians 2:15–16 and Galatians 3:10–14.

In these passages, Paul was not opposing a legalistic insistence that obedience to the law of God in general is the basis for finding favour with God. Rather, Paul was opposing the idea that the 'works of the law', observances that distinguish Jews from Gentiles, are necessary badges of covenant membership. Paul objects to the 'works of the law' that served as ritual markers of identity to separate Jews from Gentiles.[24]

---

[24] 'The New Perspective on Paul', p. 200.

A NEW VIEW OF 'JUSTIFICATION': N. T. WRIGHT

The third claim of the new perspective – that we need to redefine what Paul understood by justification – is ably set forth in the writings of N. T. Wright, the Church of England's Bishop of Durham.[25]

[25] Wright has written a number of substantial volumes in New Testament studies and in the contemporary 'third quest for the historical Jesus':

The Climax of the Covenant: Christ and the Law in Pauline Theology (Minneapolis: Fortress, 1991); *The New Testament and the People of God* (Minneapolis: Fortress Press, 1992); *Christian Origins and the Question of God,* (3 vols.; Minneapolis: Fortress Press, 1992, 1996, 2003); *Who Was Jesus?* Grand Rapids: Eerdmans, 1992.

Among Wright's works that most directly represent his understanding of Paul and the doctrine of justification are the following:

What Saint Paul Really Said: Was Paul of Tarsus the Real Founder of Christianity? (Grand Rapids: Eerdmans, 1997); 'New Perspectives on Paul'. http://home.hiwaay.net/~kbush/ Wright _New_Perspectives.pdf; 'The Paul of History and the Apostle of Faith', *Tyndale Bulletin,* 29 (1978): 61–88; 'The Law in Romans 2', in *Paul and the Mosaic Law,* ed. James D. G. Dunn (Grand Rapids: Eerdmans, 1996), pp. 131–50; 'The Shape of Justification.' http://www.angelfire.

In his interpretation of Paul's understanding of justification, Wright proceeds from the conviction that Sanders and Dunn undermined two essential features of the older, Reformation view:

FIRST, whereas the Reformation perspective assumed that Paul articulated the doctrine of justification in opposition to Jewish legalism, *Sanders' study of Second Temple Judaism has demonstrated compellingly that no such legalism was prevalent at the time of the writing of Paul's epistles.* Whatever the apostle Paul's problems with Judaism were, they were not directed against its legalism.

Wright's endorsement of Sanders' new view of Judaism and its importance for understanding Paul's gospel is clear: ' . . . The tradition of Pauline interpretation has manufactured a false Paul by manufacturing a false Judaism for him to oppose.'[26]

------

com/mi2/paulpage/Shape. html; *The Letter to the Romans,* vol. 10 of *The New Interpreter's Bible* (Nashville, TN: Abingdon Press, 2002); *Paul for Everyone: Romans Part 1, Chapters 1–8* (Louisville, KY: Westminster/John Knox Press, 2004). Wright also has a volume on Paul, *Paul: Fresh Perspectives* (Fortress, 2005), which was not available for comment at the time of writing.

[26] 'The Paul of History and the Apostle of Faith', *Tyndale Bulletin* (1978): p. 78.

Indeed, the Reformation's understanding of the gospel of free justification amounts to what Wright terms 'the retrojection of the Protestant-Catholic debate into ancient history, with Judaism taking the role of Catholicism and Christianity the role of Lutheranism'.[27]

Because the Reformation misunderstood the problem to which Paul was actually responding, it failed to grasp the real meaning of Paul's teaching on justification by faith.

SECOND, in addition to his agreement with Sanders' general description of Judaism as a non-legalistic religion, *Wright also makes sympathetic use of Dunn's interpretation of Paul's dispute with the Judaizers and their understanding of the 'works of the law'*. The problem with the Judaizers' appeal to the 'works of the law' was not its legalism, Wright insists, but its *perverted nationalism*. The Pauline expression, 'the works of the law', does not refer to a legalistic claim regarding how sinners can find favour with God by obeying the law, but to the nationalistic Jewish claim that God's covenant promise only extends to the Jews.

---

[27] 'The Paul of History', p. 80.

If we ask how it is that Israel has missed her vocation, Paul's answer is that she is guilty not of 'legalism' or 'works-righteousness' but of what I call 'national righteousness', the belief that fleshly Jewish descent guarantees membership of God's true covenant people. . . . Within this 'national righteousness', the law functions not as a legalist's ladder but as a charter of national privilege, so that, for the Jew, possession of the law is three parts of salvation: and circumcision functions not as a ritualist's outward show but as a badge of national privilege.[28]

The problem Paul confronted in his dispute with the Judaizers was a 'boasting' in national privilege, and an unwillingness to acknowledge that the covenant promise extends to Gentile as well as Jew.[29]

Before directly considering Wright's interpretation of Paul's doctrine of justification, it should be observed that he believes the doctrine of justification to be a subordinate theme in Paul's proclamation of the gospel.

[28] 'The Paul of History', p. 65. See Wright's *Romans*, pp. 139, 148–9.

[29] *What Saint Paul Really Said: Was Paul of Tarsus the Real Founder of Christianity?* pp. 128–9. Cf. N. T. Wright, 'The Law in Romans 2', pp. 139–43.

Though it is often assumed that the gospel is a 'system of how people get saved', Wright insists that this seriously misrepresents the real meaning of the gospel.[30] The gospel does not answer the question of the guilty sinner, 'How can I find favour with God?' (compare, e.g., Luther), but rather it answers the question, 'Who is Lord?'

One of the unfortunate features of the Reformation and of much evangelical thinking, according to Wright, is that they reduce the gospel to 'a message about "how one gets saved", in an individual and ahistorical sense'.[31]

In this way of thinking, the focus of attention, so far as the gospel is concerned, is upon 'something that in older theology would be called an *ordo salutis,* an order of salvation'.[32] Because of its inappropriate focus upon the salvation of individual sinners, the older Reformation tradition was bound to exaggerate the importance of the doctrine of justification.

Whereas the Reformation perspective under-stands the gospel in terms of the salvation of individual sinners, Wright maintains that Paul's

[30] *What Saint Paul Really Said*, p. 45.
[31] *What Saint Paul Really Said* , p. 60.
[32] Ibid., pp. 40–1. See also *Romans*, p. 403.

gospel has a different focus. According to Wright, the basic message of Paul's gospel focuses upon *the lordship of Jesus Christ.*

> Paul's new vocation involved him not so much in the enjoyment and propagation of a new religious experience, as in the announcement of what he saw as a public fact: that the crucified Jesus of Nazareth had been raised from the dead by Israel's God; that he had thereby been vindicated as Israel's Messiah; that, surprising though it might seem, he was therefore the Lord of the whole world.[33]

Through the cross and resurrection of Jesus Christ, the one true God, who is the Creator of the world, has won a 'liberating victory . . . over all the enslaving powers that have usurped his authority'.[34]

Though Wright does not often spell out concretely what he means by the lordship of Jesus Christ, he does offer the following summary description:

---

[33] *What Saint Paul Really Said*, p. 40.

[34] Ibid., p. 47. See also 'The Climax of the Covenant', pp. 21–26; and *The New Testament and the People of God*, pp. 244–79.

Paul discovered, at the heart of his missionary practice, that when he announced the lordship of Jesus Christ, the sovereignty of King Jesus, the very announcement was the means by which the living God reached out with love and changed the hearts and lives of men and women, forming them into a community of love across traditional barriers, liberating them from paganism which had held them captive, enabling them to become, for the first time, the truly human beings they were meant to be.[35]

The great theme of the gospel is this message of Jesus' lordship and its life- and world-transforming significance. Rather than the salvation of individual sinners, the theme of Christ's lordship is the primary focus of Paul's preaching.[36]

In order to understand Wright's interpretation of the doctrine of justification within the setting of this view of Paul's gospel, we will consider briefly several of its distinct features:

1. his interpretation of the phrase, 'the righteousness of God', as the basis for the justification of God's people;

[35] *What Saint Paul Really Said*, p. 61.
[36] *What Saint Paul Really Said*, p. 133.

2. the precise meaning of the expression, 'to justify';

3. the role of faith as a 'badge' of covenant membership;

4. the past, present and future tenses of justification; and

5. the relation between Christ's cross and resurrection and the church's justification.

1. The 'righteousness of God'

Wright's discussion of the expression, 'the righteousness of God', begins by noting that this expression would have been readily understood by readers of the *Septuagint*, the Greek translation of the Old Testament. In the *Septuagint*, the 'righteousness of God' refers commonly to 'God's own faithfulness to his promises, to the covenant'.[37]

God's 'righteousness', especially in Isaiah 40–55, is that aspect of God's character because of which he saves Israel, despite Israel's perversity and lostness.

---

[37] Ibid., p. 96. For an extended treatment of Wright's understanding of the theme of the 'righteousness of God' in Romans, see his *The Letter to the Romans*, pp. 397–405.

God has made promises; Israel can trust those promises. God's righteousness is thus cognate with his trustworthiness on the one hand, and Israel's salvation on the other. And at the heart of that picture in Isaiah there stands, of course, the strange figure of the suffering servant through whom God's righteous purpose is finally accomplished.[38]

The righteousness of God does not refer to God's moral character, on account of which he punishes the unrighteous and rewards the righteous. This common medieval idea of God's 'distributive justice' is little more than a 'Latin irrelevance'.[39] Rather, the righteousness of God is *his covenantal faithfulness in action.*

When God acts to fulfil his promises to Israel, he demonstrates or reveals his faithfulness as one who will accomplish his saving purposes on her behalf. This covenant faithfulness refers both to a 'moral quality' in God (God is *righteous*, that is, *faithful*) and to an 'active power which goes out, in expression of that faithfulness, to do what the covenant always promised'.[40]

[38] *What Saint Paul Really Said*, p. 96.

[39] Ibid., p. 103.

[40] *What Saint Paul Really Said*, p. 103. For this reason, Wright regards the traditional grammatical debate over

Though the righteousness of God is primarily to be identified with God's covenantal faithfulness in action, Wright does acknowledge that this phrase, in its Old Testament and Jewish context, makes use of a legal (court-room) metaphor.

The language of the righteousness of God derives from the Jewish idea of the law court in which three parties are present: the judge, the plaintiff and the defendant. In the law court, each of these parties has a distinct role to play: the judge is called upon to decide the issue and to do so in a proper manner, that is, justly and impartially; the plaintiff is obliged to prosecute the case and bring an accusation against the defendant; and the defendant is required to answer the accusation and seek acquittal.

What finally matters in this court setting is not the moral uprightness or virtue of the plaintiff or the defendant, but the *verdict of the judge*. When the judge decides 'for' or 'against' either the plaintiff or

---

whether the genitive in 'righteousness *of* God' is 'possessive' or 'subjective' to be beside the point. The righteousness of God is both God's being righteous (possessive) and God's acts of righteousness (subjective). God's covenant faith–fulness expresses itself in deeds performed to fulfil his covenant promises.

the defendant, we may say that they have a *status of being righteous* so far as the court's judgment is concerned. So far as the judgment of the court goes, 'the righteous' are those whom the court vindicates or acquits, 'the unrighteous' are those whom the court finds against or condemns.

Though Wright affirms the forensic nature of this language in a way that is reminiscent of the Reformation view of justification, he maintains that the Reformation's idea of the imputing or imparting of God's righteousness to believers makes no sense.

> If we use the language of the law court, it makes no sense whatever to say that the judge imputes, imparts, bequeaths, conveys or otherwise transfers his righteousness to either the plaintiff or the defendant. Righteousness is not an object, a substance or a gas which can be passed across the courtroom.[41]

According to Wright, the 'righteousness of God', which refers to God's faithfulness to the promises he made to Israel, cannot be granted or imputed to believers. Nothing like an act of imputation need occur in order for God to declare in favour of his people.

[41] *What Saint Paul Really Said,* p. 99.

45

2. What it is to be 'Justified'

In Wright's view, we can properly understand the idea of 'justification' only within the context of understanding God's righteousness as his covenant faithfulness in action. Justification is not basically about how guilty sinners, who are incapable of finding favour with God by their works of obedience to the law, can be made acceptable to God, but about *who belongs to the number of God's covenant people.*

The primary location of Paul's doctrine of justification, Wright insists, is not soteriology (how are sinners saved?) but ecclesiology (who belongs to the covenant family?). When Paul's treatment of justification is read within the context of Judaism's historic understanding of the covenant, we discover that justification 'in this setting . . . is not a matter of *how someone enters the community of the true people of God,* but of *how you tell who belongs to that community'.*[42] In a comprehensive statement of his view, Wright maintains that the terminology of justification functions to describe who belongs to the covenant people:

[42] *What Saint Paul Really Said,* p. 119.

'Justification' in the first century was not about how someone might establish a relationship with God. It was about God's eschatological definition, both future and present, of who was, in fact, a member of his people. In Sanders' terms, it was not so much about 'getting in', or indeed about 'staying in', as about 'how you could tell who was in'. In standard Christian theological language, it wasn't so much about soteriology as about ecclesiology; not so much about salvation as about the church.[43]

When God reveals his righteousness in the death and resurrection of Jesus Christ, he demonstrates his covenant faithfulness by securing the inclusion of all members of the covenant community, namely, those who are baptized into Christ and are marked

---

[43] Ibid., p. 120. See also Wright's *Romans,* pp. 465, 473, 481. Wright has a similar comment on Paul's argument in Galatians: 'Despite a long tradition to the contrary, the problem Paul addresses in Galatians is not the question of how precisely someone becomes a Christian, or attains to a relationship with God. . . . On anyone's reading, but especially within its first-century context, it has to do quite obviously with the question of how you define the people of God: are they to be defined by the badges of Jewish race, or in some other way?' (*What Saint Paul Really Said,* p. 122). Cf. Wright, 'Curse and Covenant: Galatians 3.10–14', in *The Climax of the Covenant,* pp. 137–56.

by the 'badge' of covenant membership, which is faith.

According to Wright, when the language of justification is interpreted in terms of its Old Testament and Jewish background, we will recognize that it is covenantal language. Justification does not describe how someone gains entrance into the community of God's people but *who is a member of the community* now and in the future. In Paul's Jewish context, Wright maintains,

> . . . 'justification by works' has nothing to do with individual Jews attempting a kind of proto-Pelagian pulling themselves up by their moral bootstraps, and everything to do with definition of the true Israel in advance of the final eschatological showdown. Justification in this setting, then, is not a matter of *how someone enters the community of the true people of God,* but of *how you tell who belongs to that community,* not least in the period of time before the eschatological event itself, when the matter will become public knowledge.[44]

[44] *What Saint Paul Really Said,* p. 119 (emphasis Wright's). Cf. *Romans,* p. 497.

3. FAITH, THE BADGE OF COVENANT MEMBERSHIP

Because justification focuses upon *membership* in the covenant community, Wright interprets Paul's insistence that justification is by faith and not by works, in a manner that is similar to Dunn's approach. The 'boasting' of the Judaizers was not a self-righteous pride before God, but a kind of misplaced nationalistic pride or exclusivism.

The 'works of the law' were those requirements of the law that served to distinguish Jews from Gentiles, and to exclude Gentiles from membership in the covenant community.

However, now that Christ has come to realize the covenant promise of God to Abraham, faith in Christ is the *only badge* of membership in God's worldwide family, which is composed of Jews and Gentiles alike.

Paul's insistence that justification is by faith expresses his conviction that with the coming of Christ, God is 'now extending his salvation to all, irrespective of race'.

Justification . . . is the doctrine which insists that all who share faith in Christ belong at the same table, no matter what their racial differences, as together they wait for the final creation.[45]

One of the surprising and provocative implications of this understanding of justification, according to Wright, is that it radically undermines the usual polemics between Protestants and Catholics. Whereas many Protestants have historically argued that justification is a church-dividing doctrine, precisely the opposite is the case: Paul's doctrine of justification demands an inclusive view of membership in the one family of God:

> Many Christians, both in the Reformation and in the counter-Reformation traditions, have done themselves and the church a great disservice by treating the doctrine of 'justification' as central to their debates, and by supposing that it describes that system by which people attain salvation. They have turned the doctrine into its opposite. Justification declares that all who believe in Jesus Christ belong at the same table, no matter what their cultural or racial differences.[46]

---

[45] *What Saint Paul Really Said,* p. 122.
[46] Ibid., pp. 158–9.

Protestants who insist upon a certain formulation of the doctrine of justification as a precondition to church fellowship, accordingly, are guilty of turning the doctrine on its head. Rather than serving its proper purpose of joining together as members of one family all who believe in Christ, the doctrine of justification is turned into the teaching of justification 'by believing in justification by faith'.[47]

4. JUSTIFICATION: PAST, PRESENT, AND FUTURE

One feature of the doctrine of justification that receives special emphasis in Wright's understanding is its nature as an eschatological vindication of God's people.

When God justifies or acknowledges those who are members of his covenant community, he does so in anticipation of their 'final justification' at the last judgment.

---

[47] 'The Shape of Justification', http://www.angelfire.com/mi2/paulpage/Shape.html, p. 3. This article is Wright's response to Paul Barnett's critical evaluation of his understanding of justification. Barnett is an Anglican bishop from the diocese of Sydney in Australia. Cf. 'Tom Wright and The New Perspective', http:///www.anglicanmediasydney. asn.au/pwb/ntwright_perspective.htm.

Justification occurs in three tenses or stages –
past, present, and future. The justification of God's
covenant community in the present is founded upon
'God's past accomplishment in Christ, and anticipates the future verdict'.[48]

In the *past* event of Christ's cross and resurrection, God has already accomplished in history
what he will do at the end of history. Jesus, who
died as the 'representative Messiah of Israel', was
vindicated or justified by God in his resurrection
from the dead.

Christ's resurrection represents God's justification
of Jesus as the Son of God, the Messiah, through
whom the covenant promise to Abraham ('in your
seed all the families of the earth will be blessed') is
to be fulfilled. Because that promise comes through
the crucified and risen Christ, it cannot come
through the law (compare *Rom.* 8:3).

This past event of Christ's justification becomes a
present reality through faith. All those who believe
in Jesus as Messiah and Lord are justified, that is,
acknowledged by God to be members of the one
great family of faith composed of Jew and Gentile
alike. Furthermore, because the present reality of

[48] 'The Shape of Justification', p. 2.

justification focuses upon membership in the covenant community, baptism into Christ is the event that effects this justification: 'The event in the present which corresponds to Jesus' death and resurrection in the past, and the resurrection of all believers in the future, is baptism into Christ.'[49]

Though justification has a past and present dimension, its principal focus lies in the future. At the final judgment or 'justification', God will declare in favour of his people, the covenant community promised to Abraham.

In this final justification, God's vindication of his people will even include a 'justification by works'. Commenting on Romans 2:13 ('It is not the hearers of the law who will be righteous before God, but the doers of the law who will be justified'), Wright insists that 'those who will be vindicated on the last day are those in whose hearts and lives God will have written his law, his Torah'.[50] The 'works of the law' that justification excludes are those badges of Jewish identity that served to exclude Gentiles. Justification does not exclude, however, those works

---

[49] 'The Shape of Justification', p. 2.
[50] *What Saint Paul Really Said*, pp. 126–7. Cf. *Romans*, p. 440: 'Justification, at the last, will be on the basis of performance, not possession.'

of the law that are equivalent to the obedience of
faith by the working of the Spirit.

5. JUSTIFICATION AND THE WORK OF CHRIST

One final feature of Wright's view of justification
that remains unclear is his understanding of the
work of Christ. Wright speaks of Christ's cross as a
'representative' death, and of his resurrection as his
vindication by God.

But Wright does not provide a complete account
of Christ's work of atonement in relation to the
justification of believers. One point that emerges
clearly in his limited treatment of this subject is that
he has little sympathy for the historic view that
Christ's death involved his suffering the penalty and
curse of the law on behalf of his sinful people,
whether Jews or Gentiles.

In an extended treatment of Galatians 3:10–14,
for example, Wright insists that its language 'is
designed for a particular task within a particular
argument, not for an abstract systematised statement'.[51]

Galatians 3 is not about Christ suffering the curse
of the law in the place of his people, all of whom

[51] *The Climax of the Covenant*, p. 138.

have violated the law and are therefore liable to its curse. Paul is not talking about a general work of Christ that benefits sinful Jews and Gentiles alike. The traditional reading of this passage, which takes it to refer to Christ's substitutionary atonement for Jewish and Gentile sinners, is, in Wright's view, seriously mistaken.[52]

If this passage is read in its first-century Jewish context and within the setting of God's covenant promise to Israel, it will become evident that Paul is talking about the curse of the exile that Israel is experiencing as a people: ' . . . in the cross of Jesus, the Messiah, the curse of exile itself reached its height and was dealt with once and for all, so that the blessing of covenant renewal might flow out the other side, as God always intended'.[53]

Wright's reading of Galatians 3 is characteristic of his treatment of the subject of Christ's atoning work. Though it is evident that he does not agree with the older, Reformation understanding of Christ's saving work, what he is prepared to offer as an alternative remains rather obscure.

[52] Ibid., p. 150. Wright's claim that Paul (and Second-Temple Judaism) viewed Israel as being in exile at the time of Christ's ministry is pivotal to his interpretation, though it remains controversial.   [53] Ibid., p. 141.

Christ's death and resurrection are representative of Israel's exile and restoration. They are the means whereby the promise of the covenant is now extended to the whole world-wide family of God.

However, since Wright maintains that Paul's doctrine of justification is not primarily addressed to the problem of human sinfulness and guilt, his understanding of the work of Christ likewise puts little emphasis upon the kinds of themes that historically formed an essential part of the doctrine of Christ's atoning work.[54]

Though Wright employs a range of biblical terminology to describe Christ's redemptive work, his emphasis upon the assertion of Christ's lordship suggests that his view has more affinity with what historians of doctrine term the 'classic' or 'victory over the powers' conception than the penal-satisfaction emphasis of the Reformation. Since Wright insists that the problem to which justification provides an answer is the identification of

---

[54] For a critical assessment of the way Wright treats the work of Christ as 'representative' in Romans 5:12–21, see my recent article, 'N. T. Wright on Romans 5:12–21 and Justification: A Case Study in Exegesis, Theological Method, and the "New Perspective on Paul"', *Mid-America Journal of Theology*, 16 (2005):29–82, esp. 67–72.

those who belong to the covenant, he does not articulate a doctrine of the atonement along the lines of classic Protestant theology.

4

A CRITICAL ASSESSMENT OF THE NEW PERSPECTIVE

Now that we have summarized some of the key claims of the new perspective on Paul, we return to the question with which we began this book: Is the new perspective on Paul a theological fad, which is destined to go the way of all fashions generally, or does it represent a substantial and enduring alternative to the older, Reformation perspective, clarifying the teaching of the Scriptures?

Despite the contemporary influence of the new perspectives on the teaching of Paul, I remain convinced that the older, Reformation perspective more faithfully and comprehensively represents the teaching of the Scriptures.

Despite the boldness of the new perspective's claims for itself, there are several problems with it as an alternative to the older perspective.

These problems, which we will only briefly discuss in the remainder of our study, belie the far-reaching claims that advocates of the new perspective make for their view, and illustrate why the Reformation's reading of the apostle Paul remains more satisfying and coherent.

AN EXAGGERATED VIEW OF SANDERS' ACHIEVEMENT

We have noted that many contemporary proponents of a new approach to our understanding of the apostle Paul's gospel proceed from the conviction that E. P. Sanders' study of Judaism requires something of a 'revolution' in Pauline studies.

N. T. Wright well expresses this conviction, when he asserts that E. P. Sanders 'dominates the landscape [of Pauline studies], and, until a major refutation of his central thesis is produced, honesty compels one to do business with him. I do not myself believe such a refutation can or will be offered; serious modifications are required, but I regard the basic point as established.'[55] According to

[55] *What Saint Paul Really Said*, p. 20.

the authors of the new perspective, the new view of Second-Temple Judaism calls for a new view of the apostle Paul's teaching.

Even though Sanders has mustered a considerable body of evidence to establish that the pattern of religion in Second-Temple Judaism was what he calls 'covenantal nomism', there is an intriguing 'begging of the question' that characterizes his claims and those of many advocates of the new perspective. We can bring this out in the following question:

> Could what Sanders calls 'covenantal nomism' take a form similar to what historians of Christian doctrine call 'semi-Pelagianism'?

Sanders and other new-perspective authors are fond of arguing that Second-Temple Judaism exhibits no substantial traces of Pelagianism, the idea that God's people find favour with him on the basis of their own moral efforts. Whatever the diversity of teaching and practice within the various branches and sects of Second-Temple Judaism, few if any practised a religion that was the equivalent of a kind of 'pulling oneself up to God by one's moral bootstraps'.[56]

---

[56] *What Saint Paul Really Said.*, p. 119.

The weakness of Sanders' case, however, is that he does not seriously consider whether what he terms 'covenantal nomism' could accommodate a form of religious teaching that regards salvation and acceptance with God as being based upon grace *plus good works*.

As a pattern for the religion of Second-Temple Judaism, 'covenantal nomism' is elastic enough to allow for a kind of semi-Pelagian view of the relation between God and his people.

That Second-Temple Judaism was not full-blown Pelagianism is not surprising.[57] In the course of history, Pelagianism is a 'rare bird' in the aviary of Jewish and Christian theology. Few have argued that salvation does not require the initiative and working of God's grace, but is simply based upon human moral achievement.

Where Pelagianism has appeared, therefore, it has commonly been condemned by the major branches

[57] I am aware that I am using these terms, 'Pelagianism' and 'semi-Pelagianism', in an anachronistic and somewhat inexact fashion. For my purposes, however, it is enough to recognize that there is a considerable difference between a view that ascribes human salvation to moral achievement (Pelagianism) and a view that ascribes human salvation to God's grace *plus* good works that complete or complement the working of God's grace (semi-Pelagianism).

of the Christian church. Semi-Pelagian views, however, are quite often found in the history of Christian theology. Though these views may speak of God's gracious initiative in salvation, they also insist that human salvation does not end with this good beginning. According to semi-Pelagianism, those who find favour and acceptance with God are those who freely co-operate with his grace and complement it by a life of good works that in turn merit further grace and final salvation.

Accordingly, when the Reformers of the sixteenth century opposed the doctrine of justification in the medieval Roman Catholic Church, they did not do so – nor did they claim to do so – on the grounds that it was Pelagian, as writers of the new perspective intimate. The Reformers, including Luther and Calvin, objected to the teaching that sinners are justified by God *partly* on the basis of his grace in Christ and *partly* on the basis of their willing co-operation with this grace, which includes good works that increase the believer's justification and merit further grace.

The Roman Catholic Church, whose teaching was criticized as a re-statement of the kind of works-righteousness that the early church, including Paul, opposed, was not considered Pelagian. What prompted the Reformation was the conviction that the Roman Catholic Church taught that God's grace in Christ was not a sufficient basis for the believer's acceptance into favour with God.

The parallel, therefore, that the Reformers drew between the teachings of the Catholic church and the Judaizing heresy that the apostle Paul opposed was that they both wanted to make human works a partial basis for justification, in the present and the future.[58]

The irony here is that Sanders' description of 'covenantal nomism' closely resembles a kind of text-book description of semi-Pelagian teaching and therefore may unwittingly lend credibility to the Reformation argument.

To put the matter in the traditional language of the doctrine of justification, 'covenantal nomism' fits rather comfortably with the idea that the justification of believers, now and in the future,

---

[58] Cf. Moisés Silva, 'The Law and Christianity: Dunn's New Synthesis', *Westminster Theological Journal,* 53 (1991), p. 348: 'Sanders (along with biblical scholars more generally) has an inadequate understanding of historical Christian theology, and his view of the Reformational concern with legalism does not get to the heart of the question.'

depends upon works of obedience to the law that follow upon and are supplementary to God's gracious initiative.[59] If that is the case, then what Sanders calls 'covenantal nomism' bears remarkable formal similarities to the kind of semi-Pelagianism that marked the medieval Roman Catholic doctrine of justification.[60]

Therefore, the Reformation claim that Paul was opposing a doctrine of justification by (grace plus) works may be more on target than the new-perspective authors are willing to acknowledge.

At the very least, Sanders' exposition of Second-Temple Judaism does not demonstrate the need for the kind of new understanding of the teaching of the apostle Paul that the authors of the new perspective propose.

THE 'WORKS OF THE LAW' IN PAUL'S EPISTLES

If the first claim for a new perspective on Paul's doctrine of justification is somewhat exaggerated, the

[59] Seyoon Kim, *Paul and the New Perspective* (Grand Rapids: Eerdmans, 2002), p. 65.

[60] Cf. D. A. Carson, *Justification and Variegated Nomism* (Grand Rapids: Baker, 2004), p. 544: 'Nevertheless,

second is equally so. Even though new-perspective authors have provided a helpful clarification of the particular occasion of Paul's polemic against the Judaizers, they have not demonstrated that Paul's use of the language of 'works' or 'works of the law' refers primarily, if not exclusively, to those 'boundary-markers' that distinguished Jews from Gentiles.

A historically contextualized reading of Paul's epistles does not require the conclusion that the new perspective reaches, namely, that Paul's doctrine of justification was addressed principally to Jewish exclusivism or failure to include Gentiles as heirs to the promise to Abraham.

Paul certainly emphasizes that faith in Jesus Christ is the only way to become a recipient of the covenant promise to Abraham (*Gal.* 3:10–14; *Rom.* 3:27–31). In the course of his epistles, however, Paul's teaching regarding the law and the 'works of

----

covenantal nomism as a category is not really an alternative to merit theology, and therefore is no response to it. . . . By putting over against merit theology not grace but covenant theology, Sanders has managed to have a structure that preserves grace in the "getting in" while preserving works (and frequently some form or other of merit theology) in the "staying in".'

the law' expresses precisely the themes that were integral to the older perspective of the Reformation.

Though the new perspective interprets Paul's language regarding 'the works of the law' or 'works' as being primarily restricted to the boundary-marker requirements of the law, the apostle Paul uses this language far more broadly.

No doubt the occasion for Paul's rejection of justification by the works of the law included the exclusivism of Judaizers who insisted upon obedience to the law's boundary-markers before Gentiles could be acknowledged as members of the covenant community.

However, Paul's argument goes beyond the issue of the inclusion of Gentiles by means of their obedience to these boundary-marker requirements. According to the apostle, no one, whether Jew or Gentile, can be justified by the works of the law, because no one is able to do what the law requires (e.g. *Gal.* 3:10–14; 5:2–4; 6:13; *Rom.* 2:6; 3:20,28; 4:2–4: 9:32).[61]

---

[61] For a more extended defence of this claim than that provided in what follows, see Douglas J. Moo, '"Law", "Works of the Law", and Legalism in Paul', pp. 90–99; Charles E. B. Cranfield, '"The Works of the Law" in the Epistle to the Romans', *Journal for the Study of the New*

The works of the law which are excluded as a basis for justification include any acts of obedience to any of the requirements of the law. These requirements of the law include circumcision and other boundary-marker stipulations. But they also include all the other stipulations in the law.

The reason Paul cites for arguing that no one can be justified by obedience to the law is not simply that faith in Christ is now the only badge of inclusion within the covenant family of God.

The new perspective explains Paul's opposition to the works of the law in terms of the transition that occurs in the history of redemption with the coming

---

Testament, 43 (1991): 89–101; and Moisés Silva, 'Faith Versus Works of Law in Galatians', in *Justification and Variegated Nomism,* 2:17–48. For instances of a similar, general use of the language of 'works' in Paul's epistles, see 2 *Cor.* 11:5; *Col.* 1:21; *Gal.* 5:19. For instances of this use in passages that are not universally acknowledged as authentically Pauline, see *Eph.* 2:9–10; 5:11; *1 Tim.* 2:10; 5:10, 25; 6:18; *2 Tim.* 1:9; 4:14; *Titus* 1:16; 2:7, 14; 3:5, 8, 14. Even if we were to grant the view that these latter texts are not Pauline (which we do not), at the very least they suggest that an author influenced by Paul took him to exclude all boasting in any works whatever in the matter of salvation (*Eph.* 2:9).

of Christ. Now that Christ has come, it is no longer necessary to submit to the law's boundary-marker requirements to be numbered among the people of God.

This explanation of Paul's opposition to justification by works of the law is inadequate, however. An important element in Paul's explanation of the futility of being justified by the works of the law is the inability of any sinner, whether Jew or Gentile, to do what the law requires (*Rom.* 3:19–20; *Gal.* 3:10; 5:3).

Anyone who hopes to find life and blessing before God on the basis of his observance of the law will find that this only leads to futility and frustration (*Rom.* 7:7–12; *Gal.* 3:10, 19–22; 5:1–5). Because no one does or can do what the law requires, it is impossible to be justified on that basis.

Hence Paul does oppose a form of legalism when he rejects the idea that anyone could be justified by the works of the law. The 'boasting' of Paul's opponents is not merely a pride in their identity as Jews and as members of the covenant community.

Their boasting included the idea that, as recipients of the law of God, they were able to commend themselves to God's favour and acceptance on the basis of their obedience to its requirements (*Rom.* 3:27–4:8; 9:30–10:8; *Phil.* 3:2–11).[62]

In the final analysis, the suggestion of the new perspective that the problem Paul opposed was a form of Jewish exclusivism, not Jewish legalism, cannot be sustained.

The Reformation perspective, which identified the boasting of Paul's opponents as a boasting in their own achievements under the law, continues to be a more likely interpretation of Paul's opposition to them.

The assumption of the new perspective that Jewish exclusivism represents an alternative form of boasting to that of Jewish legalism is untenable, for this boasting was intimately related to the idea that, as recipients of the law, their obedience to the law's requirements would grant them privileged status before God.

---

[62] Cf. Simon J. Gathercole, *Where is Boasting?* (Grand Rapids: Eerdmans, 2002). Based upon his study of the motif of 'boasting' in Second-Temple Judaism and the argument of Romans 1–5, Gathercole concludes that the boast was not only made in relation to others (Gentiles) but also *in relation to God,* before whom the faithful Jew expected to be vindicated or justified for his adherence to the law.

'THE RIGHTEOUSNESS OF GOD' IN PAUL

Though Wright and other new-perspective authors claim that 'the righteousness of God' in Paul refers to the faithfulness of God in fulfilling his covenant promises, this claim does not do justice to Paul's use of this expression.

Such an understanding is far too general and imprecise to capture the specific force of this language in Paul's writings. If we say that the 'righteousness of God' is his faithfulness to his covenant promises, we still need to ask: How does that faithfulness come to expression? What exactly does the terminology of 'righteousness' tell us about the way in which God's faithfulness is demonstrated?

Study of the use of this language in Paul's epistles will show that it calls attention to the *judicial* nature of God's action in securing the acquittal or vindication of his covenant people, and bringing judgment or condemnation upon his enemies.[63]

---

[63] For brief summaries of the debate on this expression that largely uphold the Reformation view, see Mark A. Seifrid, 'Righteousness Language in the Hebrew Scriptures and Early Judaism', in *Justification and Variegated Nomism,*

Consistent with Old Testament usage, the 'righteousness of God' is revealed when God, as Judge and King, acts justly in acquitting the righteous and condemning the wicked. This is apparent in the book of Romans, which is a particularly important source for understanding Paul's use of the expression, 'the righteousness of God'.

Paul's understanding of the righteousness of God in Romans includes not only the idea of God's kingly rule over his creatures through the requirements of his law, but also his just retribution against all who transgress these requirements (*Rom.* 1:18–32; 3:21–26).[64]

1:415–42; Peter T. O'Brien, 'Was Paul a Covenantal Nomist?', in *Justification and Variegated Nomism,* 2:274–6; Henri Blocher, 'Justification and the Ungodly (*Sola Fide*)', in *Justification and Variegated Nomism,* 2:473–8; and Douglas J. Moo, *The Epistle to the Romans* (NICNT; Grand Rapids: Eerdmans, 1996), pp. 63–90.

[64] For a recent treatment of Paul's understanding of the 'righteousness of God' in Romans 3:21–26, which affirms the older Reformation view and critically evaluates the view of the new perspective, see D. A. Carson, 'Atonement in Romans 3:21–26', in *The Glory of the Atonement,* ed. Charles E. Hill and Frank A. James III (Downers Grove, IL: InterVarsity, 2004), pp. 119–39, especially pp. 124–9.

Though similar expressions are used in his other epistles, this epistle is the only one to use the expression on several occasions (*Rom.* 1:17; 3:5, 21, 22, 25, 26; 10:3; eight times in all). These passages also indicate that righteousness is something that God grants to believers, and that it restores believers to favour with him. Through the response of faith, believers come to benefit from the saving power of the gospel of Jesus Christ, which reveals the righteousness of God in justly punishing sin and upholding God's law.

In Romans 5:17, for example, the 'righteousness' that acquits believers of condemnation and death is God's 'gift' to them (cf. *Phil.* 3:9). Similarly, in Romans 10:3–6, Paul draws a close parallel between the 'righteousness of God' and the 'righteousness based on faith' (*Rom.* 3:21–26; 10:3). Paul's use of the language of the 'righteousness of God', therefore, seems to warrant the Reformation view.

Against the background of the Old Testament idea of God's righteousness, the apostle Paul is affirming that the gospel of Jesus Christ reveals God's judicial action in securing the righteous status of his people before him. What is remarkable about the gospel of God's righteousness in Christ is that

God has, in the Person and work of his Son, entered into judgment on behalf of *the ungodly* (*Rom.* 4:5). All who receive the free gift of right standing with God on the basis of the work of Christ, are beneficiaries of God's righteousness. They are freed from condemnation and accepted by God, the Judge. God's righteousness reveals his covenant faithfulness to secure his people's salvation, to be sure. But it especially reveals God's powerful intervention in his own court to grant a righteous status to believers on the basis of Christ's work on their behalf.

THE NATURE OF 'JUSTIFICATION'

Though the new-perspective writers insist that the language of 'justification' is 'covenant membership' language, this view is inadequate in several respects.

Like the claim that the 'righteousness of God' refers to God's covenant faithfulness in action, such an understanding is far too general and imprecise to capture the specific force of this terminology in Paul's writings. No doubt this language finds its meaning within the context of God's establishing a relationship with those whom he acknowledges as his covenant people. But this does not yet tell us what precisely 'justification' means, and why this language is especially appropriate to describe what God does when he brings people into his covenant family.

Perhaps the most serious problem with a simple identification of the language of 'justification' with the idea of 'belonging to the covenant people' is that it fails to do justice to the biblical context for Paul's discussion of justification. If we consider only the context for the discussion of justification in Romans 1–5, we discover that justification answers to the problem of human sin and guilt before God. The problem of human sin and guilt, as Paul outlines it in these chapters, belies N. T. Wright's genial suggestion that first-century Jews were not particularly troubled by the prospect of the final judgment and the wrath of God, or whether they would 'get to heaven' in the future.[65]

Though there is an undoubtedly ecclesiological dimension to the language of justification – Who belongs to the covenant family? Are Gentiles as well as Jews included? – *the principal issue* is quite emphatically of a *soteriological* and *theological* nature. The question that Paul's argument in

---

[65] Wright, *What Saint Paul Really Said*, p. 118.

Romans 1–5 raises goes deeper than who belongs to the covenant people of God. The question raised is: How can guilty sinners, who have culpably broken the law of God and are subject to condemnation, be received into favour with a righteous God whose wrath is being poured out upon all the ungodliness and unrighteousness of men?

The importance of this context for understanding the language of 'justification' requires that we briefly review the argument of these chapters.

Immediately after Romans 1:16–17, which announces the theme of the epistle ('the righteousness of God is revealed from faith to faith'), Paul notes that 'the wrath of God is revealed from heaven against all ungodliness and unrighteousness of men' (1:18). The good news that God justifies the ungodly occurs, accordingly, against the dark background of God's just displeasure with all guilty violators of his law.

For this reason, the problem that is resolved by the revelation of God's righteousness is not whether God is faithful to his covenant, *but whether he is in the right when he justifies those who, by virtue of their sin and guilt, are worthy only of condemnation and death.* It is not God's faithfulness to his promise that is in question; rather, the question is whether human beings, who are on trial before God on account of their sins and offences, can find favour or acceptance with God.

Following the announcement of the theme of God's righteous wrath in Romans 1:18, the apostle turns in chapter 2 to the reality of this impending judgment. A 'day of wrath' is coming, when God 'will render to each one according to his works' (2:5–6). This day will reveal God's judgment by Christ Jesus upon the deeds of all, including the 'secret things of men' (2:16). The setting for the demonstration of the 'righteousness of God' and the 'justification' of believers, therefore, is clearly one of trial and judgment before God.

Within this setting of trial and judgment before God, the apostle proceeds, after the manner of a prosecutor in a courtroom, to detail the universal sway of sin and guilt among Jews and Gentiles alike. At the beginning of chapter 2, Paul hints that his Jewish readers might be tempted to affirm his indictment of Gentile sinners and offenders, while excluding themselves. However, he forcefully argues that *all* have sinned, whether they are Gentiles 'without the law' or Jews 'under the law' (2:12). Those who might be tempted to boast before God because of their privileged position, including their possession of the covenant mark of circumcision, are reminded that 'circumcision indeed is of value if you obey the law, but if you break the law, your circumcision becomes uncircumcision' (2:25).[66]

In order to prove that Jews as much as Gentiles are at no advantage before God, Paul cites evidence of an *ad hominem* nature to illustrate how they also have disobeyed the law of God. Despite their boast, they are as guilty as the Gentiles of the sins of hypocrisy, stealing, adultery, robbing temples (2:21–22). And so he draws the inescapable conclusion: 'You who boast in the law dishonour God by breaking the law' (2:23).

The significance of this setting in Romans for Paul's understanding of justification cannot be overstated. In this setting, justification does not merely refer to 'covenant membership'. After all, the Jews who were circumcised were members of the covenant people of God. Nor can justification be

---

[66] In verse 13, Paul speaks similarly: 'For it is not the hearers of the law who are righteous before God, but the doers of the law who will be justified.' As we shall see below (see fn. 68), among writers of the new perspective this text is interpreted as a positive affirmation by Paul that in the final judgment only those who do what the law requires will be justified or vindicated. Cf. Wright, *What Saint Paul Really Said*, p. 126.

reduced to Paul's answer to the question: Are Gentiles also members of the covenant family?

To reduce the problem to which justification provides an answer to the inclusion or non-inclusion of Gentiles within the covenant family is to minimize the real problem. Since no one can possibly be included within the covenant family of God on the basis of the works of the law, God has demonstrated his righteousness in providing a Saviour whose obedience and propitiatory death form the basis for the believing sinner's reception into his favour.

In the setting of the argument of Romans, therefore, justification language refers to God's act of granting believers a status of favour and righteousness on account of the work of Christ. Justification is all about the forgiveness of sins and the granting of a new status of righteousness in Christ to otherwise guilty, condemnable sinners. Paul's teaching about justification is not simply about 'who is a member of the covenant', but it goes to the deeper issue of 'who has a right to stand before God, despite his sin and unworthiness'.

Justification is about God who 'justifies the ungodly' (*Rom.* 4:5). And it is about nothing if not the *salvation* of guilty sinners. Only within the framework of these deeper theological and soter-iological issues does the obvious ecclesiological issue regarding the inclusion of Gentiles have a place.

'SUBSTITUTION', 'IMPUTATION', AND 'FAITH'

We have previously observed that one of the troubling features of the new perspective is its lack of clarity regarding the connection between the justification of believers and Christ's saving work, which includes the elements of substitutionary obedience and satisfaction for sin.

In the Reformation perspective on Paul, there is a close and intimate connection between Christ's perfect obedience, cross, and resurrection, and the benefit of free justification that derives from the union of believers with him. Christ's objective work on behalf of believers, his death for their sins and his resurrection for their justification (*Rom.* 4:25) constitute the basis for the verdict that justification declares. Because Christ, though without sin, bore the sins of his people upon the cross, and was declared righteous before God in his resurrection, believers enjoy a new status of acceptance with God through union with him.

The weakness of the newer perspective becomes apparent in the way it views the themes of faith and imputation in relation to union with Christ. In the older, Reformation view, justification involves a transaction in which Christ assumes the sin and guilt of his people in order that they might become the righteousness of God in him (2 *Cor.* 5:17; *Rom.* 8:1).

The verdict of free justification stems from God's granting and imputing the righteousness of Christ to believers. Faith is the instrument by which the free gift of God's righteousness in Christ is received (*Rom.* 3:22; 4:1–5; 5:1; 9:30–10:4; *Gal.* 2:16). In the newer perspective, this emphasis upon faith as an instrument that receives the imputed right-eousness of Christ is largely rejected. Faith in Christ is not a means to receive an imputed righteousness. Rather, faith is merely the badge that distinguishes those who belong to God's covenant family in Christ from those who do not.

The problem with this view is not merely that it does not do justice to the instrumental role of faith. It also fails to account adequately for the sub-stitutionary nature of Christ's atoning work and the way believers benefit from that work through faith.

In the perspective of the Reformation, there is a deep and necessary correlation between the themes of 'substitution' and 'imputation'.

Since, by God's design, Christ's life, death, and resurrection occurred *for* or *in the place of* his people, all that he accomplished *counts as theirs* so far as God is concerned (imputation). Christ's work on their behalf and for their benefit is reckoned to the account of believers (imputation), since it is *as though they had performed it* (substitution).[67]

---

[67] Carson, 'Atonement in Romans 3:21-26', p. 134, fn. 53, makes an apt observation regarding the connection between substitution and imputation: 'Part of the contemporary (and frequently sterile) debate over whether or not Paul teaches "imputation", it seems to me, turns on a failure to recognize distinct domains of discourse. Strictly speaking, Paul never uses the verb λογιζομαι to say, explicitly, that Christ's righteousness is imputed to the sinner or that the sinner's unrighteousness is imputed to Christ. So if one remains in the domain of narrow exegesis, one can say that Paul does not explicitly teach "imputation", except to say slightly different things (e.g., that Abraham's faith was "imputed" to him for righteousness). But if one extends the discussion into the domain of constructive theology, and observes that *the Pauline texts themselves* (despite the critics' contentions) teach penal substitution, then "imputation" is merely another way of saying much the same thing.'

When believers are united to Christ through faith, they come to participate in all the benefits of his saving work. Faith is the 'empty hand' by which believers acknowledge and receive all that Christ has accomplished for them.

To say that God grants and imputes the righteousness of Christ to believers is, accordingly, to acknowledge what is required by the doctrines of Christ's substitutionary atonement and the believer's union with Christ through faith.

A 'FINAL JUSTIFICATION' ON THE BASIS OF WORKS?

One uncertain feature of the newer perspective on Paul is the question of justification and a final judgment according to works. According to Wright, for example, the final judgment is on the basis of works and represents a kind of final chapter in the believer's justification.

Unlike the Reformation perspective that distinguishes between justification by grace alone apart from works and a final judgment 'according to' works but not 'on the basis of' works, this concept of a final justification suggests that the present membership of believers in the covenant family of

God is suspended upon a yet-future justification.[68] Whereas believers enjoy a present justification in union with Christ, they face the prospect of a future justification whose verdict depends upon the quality of their whole life of faith. Though it would not be correct to say that this idea of a future justification is a consensus opinion of new-perspective authors, it is clearly present in Wright's understanding of Paul.

In Paul's New Testament epistles, the theme of a future judgment of all human beings is undeniable. This final judgment is an unavoidable prospect for believers and unbelievers alike; all will be judged

[68] Some new-perspective authors appeal to Romans 2:13 in support of the idea of a yet-future justification ('For it is not the hearers of the law who are righteous before God, but the doers of the law who will be justified.') The Reformation reading of this text takes it as a kind of 'hypothesis contrary to fact'. Since no one is, strictly speaking, a 'doer of the law', no one is justified by the law. Or it is taken as a statement of fact, namely, that all whom God justifies he also sanctifies; in this sense, no one is justified without obeying the law by the working of the Spirit of sanctification. However, among writers of the new perspective, this text is interpreted differently. In their view, Paul is positively affirming that, in the final judgment, only those who do what the law requires will be justified or vindicated. Cf. Wright, *Romans,* p. 440: 'Justification, at the last, will be on the basis of performance, not possession [of the law].'

according to their works. Some passages in Paul's epistles speak of the final judgment in the most comprehensive terms (*Rom.* 2:5–8). In other passages, the apostle speaks of the final judgment particularly with respect to those who obey or disobey the gospel (2 *Thess.* 1:6–10). Even believers, who enjoy the grace of acceptance with God on the basis of Christ's saving work, will be subject to a future judgment.

In the case of believers, the final judgment promises the fullness of salvation, provided they continue in the course of faith and obedience (2 *Cor.* 11:15). In one of the clearest statements of a final judgment of believers, Paul declares that 'we must all appear before the judgment seat of Christ, so that each one may receive what is due for what he has done in the body, whether good or evil' (2 *Cor.* 5:10).

Whether in those passages that speak of God's judgment in the most comprehensive terms or in others that speak more particularly of the judgment of believers, it is clear that this judgment will be 'according to' works.

However, Paul's teaching on the subject of justification militates against the view that this final judgment represents a kind of concluding chapter in the believer's justification.[69] Paul's teaching that works are absolutely excluded as a basis for the justification of believers is simply incompatible with the idea that the final justification of the believer will ultimately be based upon works. Paul regards justification as a thoroughly eschatological blessing, which anticipates in the most definitive way the final verdict that God declares concerning those who are beneficiaries of the saving work of Christ.

If the believer's present justification could be completed or even undone in the context of a final justification, the gospel promise of free acceptance with God would be profoundly compromised. The notion of a final justification on the basis of works inevitably weakens the confidence that there is now no condemnation for those who are in Christ Jesus (*Rom.* 8:1). A final justification on the basis of works also undermines Paul's bold declaration that no charge can be brought against those who are Christ's (*Rom.* 8:33–34).

---

[69] Though the final judgment should not be connected with the believer's justification as though it were something that completes it, it is certainly permissible to say that the final judgment will be a public manifestation of what is now reality, but known only to faith as it looks upon the things that are unseen (cf. 2 *Cor.* 4:18).

Rather than treating the final judgment as a kind of further justification, therefore, we should interpret Paul's emphasis upon the role of works in this judgment in terms of his understanding of all that salvation in union with Christ means for believers. Because all believers, joined to Christ by faith and indwelt of his Spirit, are being renewed in obedience, their acquittal in the context of the final judgment will be a public confirmation of the genuineness of their faith.

Since believers receive Christ for righteousness and sanctification (*1 Cor.* 1:30), they are not saved without good works. Because justification is always accompanied by sanctification, the apostle can insist that only those whose lives confirm the indwelling presence of the Spirit of Christ will be saved. No one will be saved who does not exhibit the fruit of the Spirit's working in his or her life, and who does not persist in the way of new obedience.

This is the context for Paul's clear teaching that all will be judged in the future and that this final judgment will be according to works. However, despite this clear emphasis upon a final judgment and vindication that will be according to works, the grace of free justification remains the exclusive basis for the believer's confidence of acceptance with

God. The carelessness with which Wright and other writers of the new perspective speak of a final justification on the basis of works threatens a central point of Paul's gospel: that the acceptance and standing of believers before God rests upon the work of Christ alone.

5

CONCLUSION

The proclamation to the world of the gospel of Jesus Christ is the great task of the Christian church in every generation. Since the time of the Protestant Reformation in the sixteenth century, evangelical believers have confessed that a central benefit of the gospel is the free justification or acceptance of believers before God solely on the basis of the obedience and sacrifice of Jesus Christ.

At the heart of the gospel lies the remarkable news of God's justification of the ungodly (*Rom.* 4:5). God's righteousness has been revealed in the gospel of Jesus Christ, who died for our sins and was raised for our justification (*Rom.* 4:25). Though all have sinned and fall short of God's glory, the righteousness of God, which is revealed in the gospel from faith to faith (*Rom.* 1:17), grants peace with God to all who believe in Jesus Christ (*Rom.* 5:1).

The gospel of free justification and acceptance with God continues to speak with freshness and power to all human beings who need to know where they stand with God. Because of the saving work of Jesus Christ on their behalf, believers may be joyfully confident that there is 'now no condemnation for those who are in Christ Jesus' (*Rom.* 8:1).

With the emergence of new perspectives on Paul in recent decades, this older Reformation reading of the apostle Paul's doctrine of justification has come under sustained criticism. Whether the new perspective's criticisms of the Reformation view will prove enduring remains to be seen.

However, our identification of several problematic features of the newer perspective indicates that it would be premature to declare the Reformation perspective outdated. For, unlike the newer perspective, which reduces Paul's understanding of justification to the question of the identity of those who belong to God's covenant people, the Reformation perspective appeals to several broad themes in Paul's writings, as well as in the Scriptures as a whole.

According to the Reformation perspective, the most basic problem that any human being faces is the problem of his or her guilt before God. No human achievement or moral act can make amends before God for human sin and disobedience. No one can find favour with God on the basis of his or her own obedience to the requirements of God's holy law. Only the perfect obedience and sacrificial death of Christ upon the cross can satisfy the demands of God's justice and secure the believer's right standing before him.

Because the Reformation perspective on Paul builds upon these kinds of fundamental and enduring scriptural themes, I remain persuaded that the evangelical church will continue to stand under the obligation of preaching the old story of Christ's saving work, including the principal benefit of that work in the justification of the ungodly.

Though it may be admitted that the new perspective has illumined some significant aspects of Paul's understanding of the gospel, its claims to offer a more satisfying interpretation of Paul's gospel than that of the Reformation seem at best overstated, and at worst clearly wrong.

In a biblically and theologically satisfying manner, the Reformation perspective continues to capture one of the great themes of the Christian gospel: the amazing grace of God, who justifies, not the righteous, but the ungodly, for the sake of Christ.

SOME OTHER
BANNER OF TRUTH
TITLES

Also by Cornelis P. Venema:

THE PROMISE OF
THE FUTURE

A major examination of the teaching of Scripture on the future of the individual, the church, and the universe as a whole. The chief note sounded is one of hope: 'The future is bright because it is full of promise, the promise of God's Word.'

'Occasionally one reads a new book and feels instinctively that it will become a classic. Here is such a book . . . thoroughly biblical and spiritually edifying.'

FREE CHURCH WITNESS

'This is a first-rate book, highly recommended, spiritually very warming and bursting with valuable information and instruction.'

TABERNACLE BOOKSHOP

'Theologically substantial, careful in its exposition of Scripture, pastoral in approach, confessionally Reformed.'

CALVIN THEOLOGICAL JOURNAL

ISBN 0 85151 793 5
560 pp., clothbound

THE CASE FOR TRADITIONAL PROTESTANTISM
THE SOLAS OF THE REFORMATION

Terry L. Johnson

This timely piece of writing argues passionately and persuasively for a serious reconsideration of the great scriptural principles which undergirded the Protestant Reformation of the sixteenth century – principles which are the essence of biblical Christianity.

'The doctrinal treatment is superb, warming the heart of the believer with humble love and gratitude to God, while presenting any unconverted readers with a clear and powerful presentation of the way of salvation . . . this is a book we would heartily commend. Read it yourself and give copies to your friends.'

PROTESTANT TRUTH

'Real spiritual depth on every page, yet in such an accessible form.'

REFORMED THEOLOGICAL REVIEW

ISBN 0 85151 888 5
192 pp., pbk.

SYSTEMATIC THEOLOGY

Louis Berkhof

*S*ystematic Theology was Berkhof's *magnum opus.*
Into it he poured the stores of the accumulated
knowledge he had gained during a lifetime devoted
to preparing men for the ministry. His loyalty to the
well-defined lines of the Reformed faith, his concise
and compact style, and his contemporary treatment
make the work the most important twentieth-
century compendium of Reformed theology.

'Thoroughly loyal to the Bible in its completeness
. . . a reference to the textual index shows that well
over 3,000 separate texts and passages of Scripture
are referred to . . . the reader cannot fail to be helped
to a deeper understanding of biblical truth. The
Banner of Truth Trust has put us all very much in its
debt.'

AUSTRALIAN CHURCH RECORD

ISBN 0 85151 056 6
784 pp., clothbound
(not available in the USA)

THE DOCTRINE OF
JUSTIFICATION
BY FAITH

John Owen

Owen's masterly account of justification by faith, first printed in 1677, is distinguished from other classic works on the subject by its dominating pastoral concern. The core of his work is straightforward biblical exposition, massive, fresh, compelling and practical.

'I have had no other design', wrote Owen, 'but only to enquire diligently into the divine revelation of the way . . . whereby the conscience of a distressed sinner may attain assured peace with God through our Lord Jesus Christ.'

The book has been blessed in just such a way to very many since.

Volume 5 of the
Works of John Owen

ISBN 0 85151 067 1
457 pp., clothbound

JUSTIFICATION VINDICATED

Robert Traill

Robert Traill (1642–1716), the son of a Scottish Covenanting minister, was himself a fugitive, a prisoner on the Bass Rock, an exile in the Netherlands, and later a dissenting minister in London. He wrote his masterly defence of justification by faith alone to vindicate the Protestant doctrine against the oft-repeated charge that it leads to lawlessness. His work throws a flood of light on the biblical teaching.

'Passionately and persuasively refutes all the charges of his time against this doctrine . . . will greatly encourage Reformed churches to uphold, teach, and champion justification by faith.'

CHRISTIAN RENEWAL

'A very important little book. Every Christian needs to read and study it, digest its biblical message, and spread it far and wide.'

GOSPEL MAGAZINE

ISBN 0 85151 818 4
96 pp., pbk.

THE DOCTRINE OF JUSTIFICATION
James Buchanan

'This robust classic of James Buchanan on the doctrine of justification is biblical, solid and refreshing . . . We heartily welcome this book and thank the Banner of Truth Trust for its reappearance in such an attractive format, in large clear print.'

FREE PRESBYTERIAN MAGAZINE

'Every minister should have this work, and every serious-minded Christian should be encouraged to read it.'

EVANGELICAL MOVEMENT OF WALES

'If Luther was right that justification is the article of a standing or falling church, it is time that this work was read again, for we know of nothing in English on the same scale since his day.'

EXPOSITORY TIMES

ISBN 0 85151 440 5
534 pp, clothbound

For free illustrated catalogue please write to
THE BANNER OF TRUTH TRUST
3 Murrayfield Road, P O Box 621, Carlisle,
Edinburgh EH12 6EL Philadelphia 17013,
UK USA

www.banneroftruth.co.uk